W9-BXQ-341

0

From Pastor to a Psych Ward
Recovery from a Suicide Attempt is Possible
By: Steve Austin
Copyright: 2016

Also by the Author:

The Writer's Toolkit: How to Own and Craft Your Story

Dedication

Aunt Missy was my favorite aunt: tall, thin, blonde. Beautiful. She looked like she'd just walked off the set of The Dukes of Hazzard, and she had the most infectious laugh. I loved to stay at her house during the summer with my cousins, her daughters. We would play in their above-ground pool until, by the end of summer, we'd be as dark as a glass of iced tea.

The days immediately following her suicide crawled by. The days are blurred together in my memory, but the loss left a hole in my heart that only Aunt Missy could fill.

Eventually, life picked up again. Her birthday is still marked on the calendar at my mom's house, and so is the day she died, year after year. Mom goes over and visits her grave on rare occasion.But she never talks about it. She says she thinks of her sister when she sees a butterfly, but how often do you really see a butterfly?

Aunt Missy was the only person I knew with mental illness, though no one ever called it that at the time. I had never attended a funeral of a suicide victim before hers. I was fourteen, and only very old people, like Papaw Thompson, died, unless they were sick with some rare illness. I never knew a brain could be ill.

As a teenager, I expected grief to end with the funeral. At most I thought it would be a year, max, before my family got back to normal. Nobody tells you that grief can last a lifetime, and that there's nobody ever goes back to who they were before.

This book is dedicated to my Aunt Missy, and all the aunts and mothers and brothers and best friends we have lost to suicide.

Your memory lives on forever.

-Steve Austin
August 31, 2016

A Special *Thank You*

Stephanie Gates has been my editor, writing coach, and friend for quite some time. She has edited every line of this book, either as the original blog post, or as a fresh addition to this collection. Our stories are intertwined in some pretty incredible ways and I will be forever grateful for every edit, every phone call, every last-minute project, and every time she told me the hard truth.

I'm a better writer and a better human being because of Stephanie Gates.

Check out her site at http://awidemercy.com

If you need a brilliant editor, she's the best! And if you're looking for an amazing friend, she's already taken!

Table of Contents

Author's Note...

You will notice additional "white space" at the bottom of each page. This is not by accident! I'm a writer who loves to read and take notes, so this white space is my gift to readers like me.

-S.A.

To the Person Who Just Failed a Suicide Attempt

I know you.

I guess I should say I *knew* you.

It seems like a lifetime ago. Poor guy. I'm so sorry. You look really scared and so blank. So utterly confused. And you're freezing. I remember that much. Here-have another blanket. I know, right out of the warmer? *The best!*

That catheter is going to hurt like hell when he pulls it out. But he's not going to hurt you. I know you've been hurt before, but try and be kind. He's just doing his job.

What? Oh, the necklace. It's called a "giving key". Gigi gave it to me about six months after this whole nightmare. It says *Grace.* A word you know nothing about, my friend. Not yet.

You still think grace is part of an old melody you hum as you cut grass. But grace is stronger than any other force in your life. Grace is why you're still here. And grace will lead you home.

The headache? The throat that feels like razor blades? The legs that will be numb for two more days? The staring out the window, blankly? All of that is grace. It's called a second chance.

Welcome back.

I know you don't want to be here. But one day, you'll thank God you made it. You have a long road ahead of you. Counseling, intense therapy, new meds, and lots and lots of embarrassing honesty. But you will make it. You'll find a strength you didn't have: *the strength to admit you are weak.* It will make you a new person.

No, Mom and Dad aren't going to show up. Yes, that sucks worse than just about anything else that has led you to this point. Four years later, I still can't wrap my mind around that one, but the best I can tell you is that fear makes people do some really dumb and hurtful things. Even *when* they love you.

Why's your throat so sore? You should have seen the hotel room. All of the medications you took, combined with the benadryl, turned the vomit blood red. The room looked just like a murder scene and they thought you were dead. But you'll sing again one day. *Trust me.* Here's your water. Don't try to talk. It just makes it worse. But it will heal. And so will you. You'll learn what living is really like.

In the meantime, I need to tell you a few things.

Be patient with your loved ones. They are shocked, heartbroken, humiliated, and confused. Many of them are going to be incredibly patient with you. Remember that you have exposed a wound they never knew existed, both in yourself and in their own lives. Everything they thought was secure is crumpled up on a hospital bed. They need room to doubt and ask questions and feel hurt. Do your best to speak softly and listen. Know there are going to be times when they can't hear all that you need to say.

You're incredibly lucky. According to the American Foundation for Suicide Prevention, nearly 43,000 people die by suicide in America each year. And for every death, approximately 12 more attempt. Suicide respects no one. It robs families of teenagers and grandparents, steals teachers and pastors from communities, and takes mothers away from their infants. It is a gift to survive it. I know you don't feel lucky right now, but when you learn to value your own life enough to take care of yourself at all costs, you'll see how fortunate you are.

Be kind to yourself. Recovery is a long process, so please don't think you're going to leave the hospital healed. This isn't food poisoning. This is a mental illness. You'll carry it for rest of your life. But the symptoms *are* manageable, once you learn how to deal with them. And one of the biggest components of healing is self-compassion. You *have* to stop hating yourself if you ever want to truly live.

Ignore the critics. You're going to hear some pretty ugly things - both directly and through the rumor mill - about your faith, your family, your character, and your future. People are going to tell your wife to leave you. Church folks are going to turn their back on you. And some people are going to be shockingly, painfully silent, when you need to hear from them most. But those folks aren't in this room right now. You don't need their approval. Learn to ignore the haters, or their voice will choke out new life before it ever takes root.

Grace is here. Right here, in this room. You are not a lost cause, and your life isn't over. Actually, your life is about to begin. All of those years you were running and hiding and working so hard just to keep your game face on - all of that was death. What happens next is LIFE. You don't have to do anything to find grace or deserve it. You just need to accept it, to show up for it. Grace has found you. And it will not leave you in this bed.

The psych ward will be your first experience with healing, if you let it.

This book is a collection of essays that, strung together, offers a great deal of insight into my suicide attempt and the past four years of recovery. My prayer is that you can learn from my experience and that your recovery might be just a little bit easier than mine. The truth is, recovery isn't easy. But it is absolutely worth it.

Learning to Trust My Husband After His Suicide Attempt

I will never forget how cold the tile floor was that hot September afternoon as I slid down the wall of ICU room number six. "No, I did not mix up my medicine. I wanted to die. I do not want to be here anymore," was what caused me to sink to the floor. My clearest thought was how I was not enough. But if not me, how was our beautiful baby boy not enough to make him want to stay? I wondered how I could possibly face family and friends at our son's first birthday party the next day, alone. I wondered if I would spend the rest of my life the very same way.

Never would I have dreamed this would be a part of the "for better or for worse" wedding vows I uttered with every intention of living up to. I had every right to leave. To say, "This is too much. This isn't fair." My heart was torn into pieces, but no one could hear it. I knew leaving would mean I would only remember the worst of him, and I would be choosing that fate for my son, too. Even though the day was nearly unbearable, I didn't want the worst day of my life to define the rest of my life.

I made it home the next morning, held my son and cried my eyes out. Once I was able to catch my breath, I saw so much of the good my husband had already invested in him. As I peered into my son's eyes, I hoped staying was the right choice.

I have known people who stay married only for the children. That was neither my goal nor my desire. My hope was to see healing come to my entire family. I refused to stick around only for appearances. We needed a healed marriage in order to have a healed family. We started counseling sessions shortly after Steve was released from the psych ward. That first session was *so* awkward. Where do you begin? How do you tell a complete stranger your life history? Your darkest pains, your deepest regrets? And how the hell will they make it any better?

But things did get better.

Through multiple sessions, he made ice cubes from our iceberg. He made our pain digestible and gave us clear goals and practical steps to get there. The first goal: getting honest with ourselves. The twelve sessions were not enough to heal us completely, but they were a powerful start. Counseling taught us how to slow down and listen past the voice, to the intent. We learned how to process before reacting. And in my case, I learned how to react, instead of burying my emotions.

It's been four years now, since the cold tile floor and chatter of nurses in that ICU room. To say every day has been easy would be a lie. Forgiveness is a multi-step process. Each time I have intentionally made a new, happy memory with my husband, I have fought against bitterness and blame. Our marriage isn't perfect, but we are beginning to reap the benefits of digging through the nastiest parts of our souls. And we have done it together, for better or for worse.

-Lindsey Austin

What Happens When Abuse is Your First Memory?

My first memory is phallic. He was so big. Or else I was just so little. I hate to give the guy too much credit. Perverts crave that kind of attention. My mouth was level with the waistband of his navy athletic shorts, as we both stood, flat-footed in the side yard that dusky Summer evening. It must have made things quite convenient for him. Me, less than four-years-old and him, seventeen. I was clueless, but he knew exactly what he was doing.

I don't remember the gnats, but I know they must have been out that night, to add to the confusion of what was going on. There's no other explanation for my total disdain for them. What I do remember is what the head of a dick felt like against the roof of my mouth and I learned how powerful the scent of a teenage boy's groin sweat could be before I ever entered pre-school. The pink crepe myrtle desperately tried to make this scene pretty, or at least a little less horrific, but it failed miserably. I remember the incoherent chatter of my Momma with the church ladies in the kitchen and the sounds of hammering and a table saw as my dad and the neighbor man built the deck that evening. They trusted the neighbor's son to play with me. Only, it was the other way around. He forced me to play with him. I wondered how many other little boys had played with the neighbor man's son.

I was eighteen when my Mom and I talked about my abuse for the first time. I came home and asked her what she remembered. She sat down slowly, quietly at the kitchen table. She wouldn't look me in the eye. My Dad had never been one to make eye contact, but my Mom always seemed present until that moment. She told me that she didn't know anything until bathtime. She turned on the water that night and got the temperature just right and I shucked down to get in the tub and she screamed. Her shriek was short, filled with dread, and she stopped suddenly, trying not to alarm me. *Too late.*

She called my Dad into the bathroom to have a look at the red marks on my little thighs. Dad, the paramedic and Momma, the nurse. They asked me what happened, and that began a lifetime of telling this shame-filled story. I told them clearly, honestly, exactly what happened and how big the boy's tee-tee was. I don't remember much after that but Mama told me years later that when the neighbor boy came riding up on his bike the next day for his afternoon tutoring session with her, she told him to go away and never come back. She said if he ever came around again she would tell his parents and call the police. His parents were having marital problems and his daddy was an alcoholic, so Momma didn't want to rock the boat. *How kind of her.* I didn't find out Mama's response to what happened for another fifteen years, because that's how long it was before we ever talked about it again.

She told me about the year the neighbor boy started stealing her undergarments from the clothesline in the back yard and then breaking into the laundry room under the carport. How the police found garbage bags full of her panties and nighties in his room, and how the judge sentenced him as a juvenile. First-time offenders got community service. The judge also ordered him to write my mom a letter of apology. That's the year we moved out of the little house in the tiny little town. Momma also told me that day about how her grandfather had touched her and my aunt. I always knew my aunt and I had a special connection, but by the time I was old enough to have the nerve to ask about it, she had already committed suicide.

When you lose your virginity at three-and-a-half-years-old, what happens next? For me, a lower middle class boy in a tiny town in the Bible Belt, I learned to perform. I won the Halloween poetry contest in kindergarten and my family got a pizza out of it. I also sang my first church solo that year. It was in the Christmas musical at the First Baptist Church and my Momma directed me from the audience. There's still a video of it at my parent's house.

I remember being about six-years-old, and it was the first day of baseball practice. We were dirt poor but had been lucky enough to find me a pair of decent cleats at the Thrift Store, and I'm certain they were too big. Dad always picked them too big, so that I would "grow into them". He didn't have the money to buy a pair of shoes in every size. As we walked out to practice that day one of the more well-to-do moms said, *"New cleats? Where'd you get those?"* It's funny that she even noticed them. Without thinking, I responded excitedly, *"We got 'em at the Thrift Store!"* Momma would iron my clothes: jeans, shorts, and would put creases down the sleeves of my t-shirts. You name it, she ironed it. It didn't matter if we were poor and my clothes cost $0.79 off the Goodwill rack, she was determined for "her baby" to look good. We might have been poor, but we certainly weren't going to act like it.

In second grade, I received a wooden plaque with a brass plate that read, "Good Citizen of the Year" and in third grade we moved thirty miles away. We moved out of the little white house with yellow shutters and the big deck. Away from the pink crepe myrtle in the side yard and the Arkansas Black Apple Tree in the front. I cried the day my Dad picked me up in the moving van, because that little town was all I had ever known, but somehow, the logic of a third-grader said that things would be different now. Better, and somehow more free.

In sixth grade, I won the short story contest for a much larger newspaper and I became involved in the Bible study group that met weekly before school. Sixth grade was the first year we started changing out for P.E. The smell of teenage boys and the sight of half naked boys. It was awful for me, every single day. I didn't play sports and didn't understand the rules. I was called queer and fag and every other hurtful thing a twelve-year-old boy could think of. Sixth grade was also the year of my first real girlfriend. We were "going out", which meant we played the original Nintendo in the basement at my house and we sat around at her house and kissed and I remember when she sat in my lap for the first time and how when I touched her boobs, they weren't much bigger than mine.

Seventh grade was the year the buried things started to seep back up. The year my Dad started enforcing the rule that if I came home with a grade below an eighty-five, I would be grounded until the next report card came out. It was also the year I discovered porn: an addiction that would haunt me for another twenty years.

I should have had callouses on my knees after the countless times I had knelt and sobbed my eyes out for God to forgive me and re-save me and change me. I was covered in shame. Like any true addict, I didn't want to do it, but I couldn't say no to it. I learned in church that sin is constantly waiting outside our door, ready to pounce and that at some point, our conscience is seared and we no longer care any more. I lived in constant fear that one day I would reach that tipping point and there would be nothing Jesus could do for me. I worried every night that if I died, I would burn in hell for eternity because of my dirty little secrets. But even the fear of hell could not keep the teenage boy with a gross lack of self control from filling his mind with images that no one in the Bible Belt was talking about. I even confessed my sins and filth and absolute addiction to masturbation and porn to my youth pastor. He prayed and believed for the blood of Jesus to heal me, but there were no practical steps to walk away from such a powerful addiction. And it was truly an addiction. I never questioned that fact. That was the last time I talked to anyone at the church about my struggle. Sexual sin carries with it a lie that says, "With this adventure, you can be taken away for a while. Come away with me. Let's have fun. Let's get away from it all."

As an older teen, anxiety first presented for me as perfectionism. Any grade below an 85 meant I would be grounded when I got home and I took that high bar and applied it to every possible area of my life. But in real life, no one gets above an 85 every single time. While I couldn't be perfect, I could always perform. I was the life of the party, the loudest laugh, the one who always pushed the envelope to get a response from the crowd. Inside, I was mostly miserable and empty.

As the years progressed, I continued with that *fake it to make it* mentality. I wasn't perfect at everything, but I stayed so busy that no one had time to notice. I'll never forget the day, my senior year of high school, when we went on a tour at the Department of Human Resources. I was a member of the highly selective *Youth Leadership: Shelby County*. My peers and I, along with our sponsors and various social workers were sitting around a long wooden conference room table. The concrete block walls made it cold and I wondered how any child could feel comfortable there.

I quickly realized just how uncomfortable things could become when the counselor who was leading our tour brought out the dolls they used when a child had been abused. She started talking about how they used them to let a child point to places that had been touched or violated, and my palms began to sweat. There were no words for the knot in the back of my throat or the pain in the pit of my stomach. Her words blurred in my ears and my chest grew tight. All of a sudden I was 3 years old in the side yard of my childhood home again. As I slid down the wall in the hallway of the DHR, my mind flooded back to my very first memory. It was my first panic attack.

The summer after my freshman year of college, I was a counselor at the weeklong Boy's State program at a local university. I'll never forget laying in bed on my twin mattress in the dorm room I was sharing with another college student who was serving as a counselor. I could hear him breathing heavily in the bed next to me in the middle of the night and when I saw his sheets moving up and down near his waist, I said, "Hey bro, what are you doing?" in a nervous tone. He acted like it was no big deal and said, "Let me know if you need any help over there." The next morning, I faked sickness and left the program. It was an honor to be invited as a leader, but I couldn't take living with a total stranger for a week and being involved in his sex life in any way. So I did what came so natural by this point. I ran.

That was the same year the Catholic Church's sex scandal broke. The guy who molested me wasn't a bishop or a priest. He didn't have a degree in theology and he hadn't grown up as an altar boy, but he hurt me just the same. He stole my innocence. My entire life had been marked by sexuality. He wasn't clergy. He was the white trash, redneck neighbor, who lived in the trailer across the street. And just like all those little Catholic boys, my secret was brushed right under the altar. Watching those trials was surreal. I couldn't believe it was true, yet I had witnessed the brokenness of man first-hand. I wanted to scream "me too" but I didn't know that was allowed. I wanted to hug them, to befriend them, to tell them I knew how they felt, but I didn't know people talked about issues like this. No one had ever given me permission. It wasn't until I was thirty-two years old that a friend said to me, "We can spend a lifetime hiding our secrets or supporting each other. We cannot do both."

What happens when abuse is your first memory? It changes who you are. But I think we have this beautiful picture of grace and then condemn ourselves for being human. Once I truly came to the end of myself, I began to find my true self. I have found the Love that pushes me to be my truest self, my best reflection of God. I have found the Love that is a belonging, a safe place, a fierceness that will not let me go. I have learned to find the beauty in imperfection and revel in it and I have learned to enjoy silence. God let me live and find the life I didn't even know I had.

Here is my story.

Choosing to Die

At one point, I was a youth pastor, professional sign language interpreter, wedding photographer, radio host, husband, and father. *In that order.* As an interpreter, I worked full-time in a public school, including all of my student's after-school activities. My radio show consumed Tuesday and Friday nights. Wednesday nights and all day Sunday were eaten up by church functions, and Saturdays were spent photographing weddings, with youth group activities, or both. Long days and late nights were the norm. People wondered how I could keep so many plates spinning. In my religious fervor, I judged their lack of busyness. In my corner of the Deep South, the only thing worse than a Democrat, is a lukewarm church person. I believed that lie.

My wife pleaded for attention, my friends constantly complained that I was MIA, and my anxiety was through the roof. But what could I possibly do about it, other than pop a little white pill and hope nobody discovered how badly I needed medication to get through my day. I only took my pills in the bathroom stall at work. I kept the prescription bottle hidden inside my lunchbox. As a youth pastor, I could only imagine the horrible things people would say about my lack of faith if anyone knew I was taking medicine for a mental illness. Like so many others, I didn't think I could be Christian and have a mental illness. Where I come from, mental illness is considered to be a form of demon possession. I felt stuck. Lost. The shame was nearly as unbearable as the panic attacks. They started when I was 24 and would show up once, maybe twice per month, but with this rapid pace I was trying to keep, by the time I was 28, they were weekly at a minimum.

I'd been raised in the evangelical church and laziness was the first lie I believed. The second was that I couldn't be a Christian and still have a mental illness. And the third was this: it was my job to save the whole world. If not me, then who? *Souls* were at stake! We were taught that lives were hanging in the balance of God's fiery judgment. Who could possibly sleep when "the blood of someone's eternal torment" would be on my hands? The guilt, shame, and fear I carried in the name of religion would have confused any God-fearing churchgoer.

I had completely missed the point. I had no idea that my greatest calling was to love my neighbor *and* myself. I failed to see the great responsibility of cultivating a relationship with my wife and my children. I missed the part about resting. Every night, my wife would lay next to me, longing for intimacy, for deep conversation, for friendship with the one who had promised to cherish and respect her, but I was lost in connection on my iPhone, a million miles away, planning the next youth rally or night of worship. Nothing could possibly be more of a priority that evangelizing the lost souls of Central Alabama who would obviously never hear the Good News without my help.

I figured my wife must be so proud. Look at all I was doing for the church! Yet, in having no personal boundaries, I was building walls. I was keeping the people who loved me the most at a distance. I didn't know it was okay, and even appropriate, to tell others, "no". To schedule a day off. To turn off my phone. To spend my evening with the ones who longed for my affection and attention more than I could possibly understand.

Our second ministry job was a Southern Baptist church in tiny country town. I was still working in the school system during the day and saving souls at night. Like any young youth pastor, I focused on concerts, speakers, drive-in movies, and close-knit relationships with the teens I had been called to serve. I was quickly asked to create a youth worship team to lead the Sunday night song service for the adult congregation. I was thrilled. After a year, I was beginning to be treated as a peer by the pastor. Parents and grandparents were even warming up to my less-than traditional ways. I felt accepted, like I finally had a place where I belonged.

My wife and I served together and absolutely loved sharing the message of God's grace and unconditional love. I had a successful blog, a radio show, and my whole identity was in telling kids that no matter where they'd been or what they'd done, God had an incredible plan for their lives. I blogged for XXXChurch and People of the Second Chance and found so much freedom in sharing portions of my story. But I was always still that same, broken guy, now with a wife and a little boy of my own. I had just buried things deeper and ministry was my new escape. I'd completely immersed myself in the work of the church to avoid dealing with my own issues.

I remember the day at work when I was eavesdropping on a high school conversation. An openly gay boy, talking to a high school senior who was eleven weeks pregnant. The boy asked, "How awkward was it [telling your parents]?" And she responded, "Daddy threw a couple of things and cussed me out. He told me to get out of the house." Then they made some small talk, and when I tuned back in, she said, "I had to quit softball. My life is over. Now I have a new life to care about."

Those were the kids I had such passion for. The kids I wanted to tell about the real Jesus. Those kids had grown up in a rural town much like my own hometown, where the Baptist and Methodist churches held the corner market on religion. They knew about rules and regulations and probably had mamas, just like mine, who had ironed their t-shirts as little kids. Mamas who were so hell-bent on looking good that anything ugly was never discussed. I so badly wanted to tell them about the Jesus who stopped at the well of a Samaritan woman because he was physically thirsty. The Jesus who would sweat in the Alabama sun. Those are the kinds of kids I gave my phone number to and "friended" on Facebook.

My methods were out-of-the-box and the youth room was packed week after week. I'll never forget how good it felt to have one of the youth tell me, "You're the best friend I've ever had." I couldn't imagine there being anything better, even if that student was seventeen and I was a twenty-eight-year-old, married youth pastor. Even if I was already a father to my own infant son. I had no clue what appropriate boundaries looked like. I had no real oversight and had never been told about red flags or where to draw the line with conversations with teenagers. I was changing lives for all eternity and I couldn't imagine that there was a thing in the world wrong with my methods.

I know now I was doing all the wrong things for all the right reasons. My beliefs were pretty conservative but my methods were liberal - reckless, even. I was having the conversations with broken kids that no adult had ever been willing to have with me. And I would quickly learn that no adult wanted me having those conversations at all.

It was mid-September. I was interpreting a highly confidential government assignment as my day job for two weeks. I was staying about two hours from home. I hated living in a hotel room, but after being put on administrative leave from my last interpreting job suddenly, with no explanation, I was thankful for the work. "Don't call us, we'll call you," was what I was told. One day, while out of town, I got a text message from the children's pastor at my home church. He had become a personal friend and his message said, "Stop whatever you're doing and call me". The text message made my stomach drop. I wondered what tragedy had occurred. I had no idea it would be my very own un-doing. When he answered the phone he said, "Two moms from your last school just left the church in a tirade. There's talk of you being let go from the church, too. Something about inappropriate text messages with students."

I couldn't breathe. I sank to the sidewalk outside this government building, knees like jello and heart heavy. I hadn't done anything wrong. I knew I hadn't. I had no doubt I was innocent, but just weeks before, a former fourth grade teacher from my elementary school had been indicted for inappropriate sexual contact with his students. His face was all over the cover of every newspaper in the State. All I could see was my face right there in his place. Me, the young, energetic, good looking, youth pastor and former school board employee. No one would believe a guy like me. My in laws would disown me and my wife would think I was a queer, just like those boys in middle school had called me for so many years. Shame grew quickly as all my worst nightmares were coming true. In my anxious mind, my world was crumbling. But how could I possibly escape? I felt hopeless, wishing I could wake up from this horrid nightmare, but somehow convinced this would follow me the rest of my life.

I was going to be viewed as no better than the teenage boy in the side yard, who robbed me of my own innocence. A pervert. A freak. A predator. I had been secretly addicted to pornography since I was twelve years old. I felt I had no place to give anyone hope of finding freedom because I had never tasted freedom myself. I viewed myself as an addict. A dirty, no-good, hypocrite. And I thought everyone else would be ready to burn me at the stake.

I went home that weekend and carried that sick feeling in the deepest part of my gut. My wife and I met with the pastor from the church and he cried, sitting across from us in his office. "I read the text messages," he said. The Board wouldn't let me stay without a full investigation. Lindsey wanted to know more information about the texts. "Steve didn't do anything illegal but it could be argued that he was unethical."

He knew Lindsey and I were trying so hard to reach those kids, but he also knew I was a spitfire, a loose cannon, always looking for ways to connect, to be relevant and cool. Behind the pastor's eyes, for the first time, I felt that maybe he wasn't as stiff as his suit, but yet, he didn't stand behind me. I sensed that he was struggling as much as I was in the moment. My willingness to go for the shock factor was my ultimate downfall and I see now that my jokes and conversations crossed the line. I had screwed up. There was such tension in the air as he delivered the news that I was terminated. And so were my hopes of changing the world. My ministry and my life was over.

I left home that Sunday night, headed back to my out-of-town interpreting assignment, knowing it would be the last time I would see my wife and baby boy. His first birthday was the following weekend, but I wouldn't be there to celebrate. I would forever be labeled a failure and a freak and I couldn't possibly force Lindsey to choose either to divorce me or live through the humiliation of court proceedings and a media frenzy. In the moment, I wasn't sure if I was completely insane or absolutely desperate, but I was fully aware of the failure that would forever mark my life and I chose to die anyway.

I decided to end my life a week before I actually attempted suicide. Friday morning, the last day of the assignment, one of my clients became worried when I didn't show up for the assignment. She had come to know me as a friendly guy with a larger-than-life personality, who was on top of the world. She had no idea I was feeling like the world was on top of me. This client started sending texts and making phone calls until eventually someone reached my wife, who was dumbfounded.

When the police and paramedics opened the door, they pushed through the lounger, the kitchen and coffee tables, and found my body there, in the hotel room. I was lying on my back, covered in vomit. There was vomit on the bed, on the floor, and it had projected up the wall behind me and covered a massive picture that hung behind the bed. Those who found me thought it was a murder scene. Apparently the pink Benadryl pills, along with the tens of thousands of other milligrams of prescriptions and over-the-counter medications I took, made it look like blood. They thought I was dead and I should have been. I wanted to be. I had been unconscious nearly twelve hours.

I woke up in a fog like I've never experienced before. *Where the hell am I? Why is it so cold in here? Who in the world is...wait. That's my wife and there's her best friend. Wait a second! Am I in the hospital? Shit! I'm still here? You've got to be kidding me! Am I in some sort of evil dream space, suspended somewhere between life and death? You cannot seriously mean that I didn't succeed! Do you know how much I took?! Oh this bad. This is really bad.* I was coming in and out. I remember our friend saying, *'Hey bud"* in the most fragile tone I'd ever heard her use. All I could muster was the strength to say *"Hey"* back. The next time I opened my eyes, I remember my wife standing there with a nurse and her asking me, *"Baby what happened? Did you get your medicine mixed up?"* I tried to scream, wondering why my throat hurt so bad. *"No! I didn't mix anything up! I tried to kill myself! I don't want to be here!"*

I don't think I had ever screamed at her before, up to that point. For the first several years of our marriage, we were so stuck on pleasing one another and doing things different from what we had seen with our own parents, we both held so much inside and buried it down deep. Lindsey's childhood was riddled with the affairs of her alcoholic father and eventually her mom followed suit. I could never say difficult things because she heard the voice of her father, the voice of criticism she feared so much, even though criticism was rarely my intent. And the poor girl was married to a guy who had been secretly hooked on porn for nearly twenty years. The next thing I knew, she was slumped over against the wall, in a pool of tears, apparently on the phone with her Dad, telling him I had attempted suicide. I stared out the window of my ICU room. It wasn't only my legs that were numb, apparently it was my heart too. I couldn't feel a thing.

The one flash I have of coming to was being transferred by the medical personnel from the gurney to the hospital bed. Everything was colored white except the navy of the nurses scrubs. I'm assuming it was in the ER. I remember them cutting my clothes off and it was all like a nightmare. I couldn't respond but I remember them counting "1...2...3..." before lifting me up and over. And what emotion do I remember from that? Shame. Ashamed of being naked. I had never been more vulnerable. I couldn't process all of this in that brief moment, but here I was, a failed minister, an embarrassment to anyone who ever cared about me, and I couldn't even get a suicide right. The same thing happened when the male nurse came in the next day and I woke up in one of those momentary fogs. I wasn't worried about the pain of him ripping out the catheter. I had experienced far greater pain. It was the shame attached to being naked and having my penis touched by another man. A stranger.

When Lindsey and Gigi returned to the ICU room after retrieving my belongings from the hotel room, I saw lightning flash across Gigi's eyes and for the first time in my life I knew what every country preacher I'd ever heard meant when he railed on about "righteous indignation" as he slammed his fist into the pulpit. But this was different; Gigi was furious with love for her friend. "If you ever force me to retrieve your belt from the place where you've tried to hang yourself ever again, you better hope you die. If not, I will make sure they bring you back to life, so I can kill you myself." Tears streamed down her face as she held my hand ever-so gently. She had been our closest family friend for several years.

After three days in ICU, the doctors decided my liver wasn't going to fail, and I had regained feeling in my legs. I was released from ICU and immediately transferred to the psych ward. *The psych ward.* Me. The former worship leader. The youth pastor. The Christian radio host. The blogger. The ministry school graduate. The father. The husband.

The outgoing one. The friendly one. The upbeat one. Me. I was sitting in a wheelchair, headed to the psych ward. And I stayed there for several days.

The Psych Ward and the Church

A few days later I was transferred to a psych ward. I called it the arts and crafts floor: we colored, ate, talked, and rested a lot. The days I spent in there felt pointless, frustrating, and humiliating.

I had a similar perspective of church for several years. I wondered what we were actually trying to accomplish. Sunday School curriculum felt disconnected from real life. We would dress up, sing a few songs, shake some hands, put money in a plate, listen to a professional, and go home to repeat the predictable and well-worn patterns as the week before. Why did any of it matter? Where was the life change?

After coming to the end of myself, I see how the church and the psych ward have several similarities and benefits.

They both understand the necessity of community. Think about this for a second: my life was changed by living in community – even for a short time – with unstable people at the lowest point of their lives. We came together for the social support of a safe place, and we shared a common goal. We all needed to get better. In the psych ward, our stories mattered, mutual support mattered, and finding our new normal mattered, but none of it was possible without the emotional safety we offered one another.

The same is true of the church.

Just as intake at the psych ward didn't magically change my issues or perspective, paying my tithe or showing up every week didn't bring me closer to faith on it's own accord. **I had to become invested in the process in order to find any personal benefit.** In order to change my life, I had to answer the therapist's questions honestly, figuring out how to piece a thousand fragments back together. In the same way, church did not instantly remove all of my doubts or struggles. But respecting the process and being honest about my issues with people I trust is shame-shattering. Accepting God's grace for my own journey, past and present, has helped my soul find rest. In recognizing I have problems just like the person in the pew next to me, and asking for practical ways to work through them, I am finding true healing.

I am also finding that **not everything at the psych ward applied to my specific experiences. It's true with church, too.** Not every sermon pierces my soul and not every program connects with me, but not every moment is about me. If I were to walk away from either one just because I am not catered to each and every time the doors open, I miss the point entirely.

As the nurse wheeled me down the long and lonely corridor and through the locked doors of that ward, I felt hopeless and humiliated. But on the other side, I found help for my anxieties, rest for my soul, and practical ways to walk toward my new life. On my own, without the hope Christ brings, I also find myself at the end of the rope, but in the context of healthy community, wrestling alongside others who have their own burdens to bear, I know I can keep going.

In both situations, I have found that **outward exercises are not the end game. They are designed to lead us toward inward discovery.** It's not about raised hands on a Sunday morning any more than it's about construction paper and glue stick collages of images that make me happy. Instead, the exercises are about disconnecting from unrealistic expectations, finding joy in ordinary moments, and giving ourselves space to love, belong, and constantly change. **The psych ward changed my life. And so has the Church of Jesus Christ.**

How Counseling Saved My Life and My Marriage

Flashes of light, incoherent chatter. Nothing made sense. I had done everything I could to make sure I never woke up again. So why was I here? Yet, even in such a dark moment, I felt the force of shame in my gut as the cool air hit my bare skin. Why are they touching me?! I wanted to die. **I felt ready to die.** I was overwhelmed with life and the way things seemed to be crumbling around me.

The strange thing is, I was not ashamed of trying to kill myself. It went much deeper than that. I was ashamed of being seen. The nurse cut off my clothes in the ER, while others transferred my body from the gurney to a bed, and **I was flooded with more shame than I can ever remember in a single moment**. It's literally just a flash of memory. The next second, I was out again. I stayed unconscious for several more hours as my liver decided if it would keep me alive or not. But in that space between semi-consciousness and near-death, knowing that strangers could see my body tapped into the shame of childhood abuse, and caused a great deal of panic. Even though I was barely alive.

The woman caught in adultery must have felt the same shaky tenderness the day after she wasn't stoned to death. The day after the Healer, the Rebel, the Wild Man, the Rabbi stepped into the path of her near-death moment, and told her she would not be condemned.

A stoning would be a terrible way to die. The condemned person, buried up to their waist, watched and waited as a crowd approached. The temperature below ground was below 60 degrees. Participants brought stones the size of plums.

A single hit probably wouldn't kill someone, or even knock them out, but a hundred stones nearly the size of a fist over a period several hours would do the trick. Organs would rupture and bruise and eventually begin shutting down, but the sinner remained conscious. Hurting. Aware of every blow, yet unable to run. Fully aware that life was over, unable to save themselves. It would have taken four or five hours to die.

If you ask me, **a stoning sounds a lot like how shame feels.**

For years, my life was marked by shame and fear. It's true for most victims of childhood sexual assault. I feared turning into my abuser, or realizing I was gay. And in the day-to-day, I feared the person closest to me: my wife. I was terrified Lindsey would discover just how screwed up I actually am, and decide I was not enough. Not man enough. Not strong enough. Not healed enough. Not committed enough. Not holy enough. Not sane enough. Not enough. I was scared that I would be unfaithful to her. I was scared of all of it. **As irrational as it is, I would have rather died than face my shame.**

Little did I know, my wife would be the tangible grace of God to me.

After my life fell apart and I tried to die, my wife stayed with me. Stuck with me like glue. When I had given up on myself, her faith in me became stubborn. Her trust in God is strong as steel. Others didn't understand, couldn't understand, or didn't care. But Lindsey climbed down into the muck with me and refused to let me go. It wasn't easy. Wading through that mess never is.

Shame has a way of choking the living right out of life.

After I was released from ICU and the psych ward, Lindsey and I decided if we were going to stay together, we'd have to see a therapist. It was one of the best decisions I have ever made. Therapy saved our marriage and my life. I should have been seeing a therapist for decades. I learned many things during the intense first few months of counseling but what sticks out the most is that our issues centered around a lack of trust and an abundance of shame. The problem wasn't only my failures or lack of boundaries before the attempt; the real problem was that after the attempt, she didn't know if she could trust me to be there when she needed me. If the shit hit the fan again, would I run? Could she trust me to be who I said I was and do what I said I was going to do? It all boiled down to trust.

The day the therapist helped connected all my dots back to the day I was molested, my whole world changed. When I was able to put a name to it and begin studying shame and the effects it had on every area of my life, I began to heal. That healing is still happening. I have learned that redemption is immediate but restoration is a patient process. Childhood trauma sucks, but I have learned that we have no place for shame. I have learned to address issues, not repress them. I have also learned that the Church gets it wrong so often in regards to sin. Sin is a cause for healing, not punishment. The Church also gets it wrong in regards to boundaries and oversight. I am not a predator. I wasn't ever a predator. I was a young guy with a lack of boundaries who made some stupid mistakes; however, in all of that, I know that it wouldn't be wisdom for me to put myself in that place again. My role is to take care of myself and my family and to write about my journey of faith as a broken person. I'm broken, but now I'm more okay with that fact than ever.

These days, I do a lot of wrestling. I wrestle with my faith and my wife. Wrestling is good. As we dig things up, we talk about them. We never wrestled before. People thought our individual lives and our marriage were perfect and I wouldn't go back to that place for all the money in the world. People will watch your marriage. People will judge your marriage. People will typically always believe a rumor before they believe the truth, but there is nothing in this world that matters less than the opinion of an ignorant fool and there is nothing in this world that matters more than what you have in your intimate relationship with your partner. If someone isn't sleeping with you, their opinion doesn't matter. My wife and I have been through hell and back and still have to face the gossip and criticism of others, but we continue to wrestle with God and one another and nothing in this world will ever tear us apart.

For years, I made perfection my goal. Now, I am learning to embrace the fact that I am an imperfect being, living in a broken world. What if we embraced His perfection in the midst of our imperfection? What if we accepted the fact that we are human and stopped this masquerade? We are all flawed, full of blemishes and will continue to make mistakes on a regular basis, but our brokenness is what draws us to one another.

It seems so easy at times, just to slap a bandaid on an issue and try to move forward, but eventually that bandage is going to rot, you're going to get dirt under it, it's going to fester, and you're going to be in a much worse situation that you could have possibly imagined. Healing comes through the completed work of Jesus Christ and Him alone. In no other name will we ever find healing, but healing is a process that begins with a simple, "Help me."

My life today is more open and more hopeful than it was. I hid the abuse for so long and my unintentional habit is still to hide. My gut response is to escape. To not show up. **But the grace of God calls forth courage**, and I practice forming the new habit of opening myself to safe people, creating practical boundaries, and intentionally loosening the grip of shame, a little at a time. For me, for my wife, and for our children.

Much like Jesus with the woman caught in adultery, Lindsey stepped into the circle with me. She recognized my shame and fear. She knew my painful secrets. **In the face of shame, my wife became the voice of grace.** She dared anyone holding stones to first look in the mirror before they threw the first at me. When others pushed me out, she pulled me closer. Grace has a way of doing just that: **when judgment divides, grace draws near.**

Choosing the path of unconditional love wasn't easy for my wife, but she did it anyway. When others refused to listen, she whispered, "Come home." That is the picture of grace.

Perfect love casts out all fear. And grace destroys shame.

Figuring out the winding, ruthless road of mental illness all on your own is nearly impossible. After my suicide attempt, spending time with a professional saved my marriage and, ultimately, my life.

What if the Prodigal Son Had Xanax?

Since I've begun sharing how I went from a being a pastor to being hospitalized in a psych ward, people often ask about my recovery. Everyone wants to know, is there a single solution? Where does the magic lie? How do they get their own lives (or their loved ones') back? Or, as others have said, "What is the one thing that made you want to start living again?"

The truth is, there's no magic formula, but I have learned a few intentional steps along the way, which have made my life better. I'm not a professional therapist, and everyone has a different recovery story. I can only share from my own experience.

For me, the first step was medication. If I had cancer, you can bet I would take chemo. I might also listen to the naturopath's advice to drink special juices and cut out refined sugars, or to follow the path of meditation to wholeness. But I would still take chemo.

Mental illness is a real thing. A disease. When the doctor says the chemicals in your brain aren't firing correctly and a certain medication will help level you out, listen to the doctor. It took a few tries to find the meds that were right for me, but it's worth the hassle. Some made me too sleepy, some made me too grumpy, but eventually we settled on meds that helped me find my new normal.

Again, I'm no professional, but don't rely on your primary care physician to help you sort out the complicated maze of mental health. You wouldn't go to your family doctor for cancer treatment, so why would you do that for psychiatric needs?

Anxiety has been my constant companion for as long as I can remember. For several years, I lived under a cloud of shame because of it. I believed I would never find true belonging if anyone knew the real issues I faced on a daily basis.

Until I could no longer hide. A failed suicide attempt forced me to face myself. At first, all I wanted to do was disconnect from anyone and anything that seemed more "normal" than me. And everyone seems more normal than you feel when you've just been discharged from the psych ward. I didn't want anyone to know my story, or the details of the journey that eventually landed me in an ICU. I didn't want my family to know, and I certainly didn't want to face the Church.

Like so many others, I thought life came with two choices: be a normal Christian guy, or be crazy. I felt stuck. Lost.

I wonder if the Prodigal Son was feeling like me. The parable certainly implies he was humiliated. If the Prodigal Son had been able to work through the smothering lies that come with shame, would he have come home sooner? I've heard others ask it this way: "If the Prodigal Son had Xanax, would he have ever come home?"

Early in recovery, my biggest struggle with returning to the Church was getting past that sense of not being good enough. My fear of being compared to all the other "normal" Christians made it very hard to believe in a Father who was inherently good, patient, and kind.

The Church had been my home for nearly three decades, but after such a massive personal failure, I wasn't sure how I fit into it anymore. From my own experience, the Church knows how to deal with addiction, adultery, and anger. But mental illness dumbfounds them.

I am from a spirit-filled church, where we believe in anointing oils and prayers of faith. In this world, medication for emotional issues is not really accepted. I can talk about addiction, but if I mention medication for mental illness, a team of people preps to cast out a demon.

Nearly four years into recovery, I often wonder if we would have the same response to a Christian with cancer? Sweet older women think they're being encouraging when they tell you the freedom that Jesus can bring, so you'll no longer be dependent on medication. But their message just causes our shame to simmer even more.

With both mental illness and cancer, you can't see the disease. But, while it is perfectly ok for a cancer patient to have chemo, it is not always acceptable for someone with a mental illness to take a prescription to address the chemical imbalance that dramatically affects their life. I long for the day when I can comfortably say, my hope is built on nothing less than Jesus' blood and good prescription drugs.

As it stands, the Church's response ostracizes people who need faith and community the most. Even well-meaning pastors, offering a prayer of faith at an altar call, will say God can "heal the minds" of those with anxiety and depression. Even if God can, this kind of talk just makes us want to slink back into the shadows and disappear. Healing sounds so great, but comfort and inclusion sound even better. The Church's attempts to encourage or heal are actually causing even more shame for a person who already feels they are not enough.

I want the Church to do more. That might include some research, definitely some reaching out. What would happen if the Church said to those with mental illness: you are different, but not less? What if the Church could break down walls of shame and begin a healthy dialogue? Isn't that what every person wants – to be heard and respected? To feel as though we belong?

In my experience, mental illness causes a person to look at a certain point in time thru a zoom lens. As emotions go up, rational thinking goes down. As the Church, this is the perfect opportunity to offer some of that "peace that passes understanding" to someone who feels the constriction of anxiety around their throat. Helping someone who is panicked to slow down, look at the larger picture, find God in the ordinary moments, and see all they do have to be thankful for just might save a life.

If the Prodigal Son had had Xanax, would he have come back home? Maybe so, maybe not. Or maybe he would have never left at all. Maybe he would have been able to steady his mind long enough to recognize how good his life already was. Maybe he would have thrown his arms around his dad and joined him in work, rather than floundering and acting so impulsively.

It is impossible to think about a hopeful future and a caring support system when we feel ostracized and defensive. The Father is standing, arms wide open, waiting to embrace all of His children who are burdened, weary, and anxious. It's time for the Church to stop acting like the older brother, and instead, embrace those who have wandered home after a long journey.

You Don't Owe Anyone An Apology

I'll never forget my first at-work panic attack. I was a dispatcher in a 911 call center. Everyone there knew my Dad, who is a career firefighter and EMT in the same town. I didn't know what was happening at first. In the middle of a call, my heart started racing, I felt extremely dizzy, and my hands were sweating. My chest grew tight and I couldn't respond to the emergency caller on the other end of the line. My partner looked at me and said I was really pale. The supervisor grabbed my headset and told me to go to the bathroom.

I locked the stall door (bad idea) and pulled off my shirt. I sat on the toilet and wasn't sure if I was going to throw up or what, but my stomach was churning.

I became so desperate that I finally laid down in the fetal position, my bare skin against the cold tile floor of the office bathroom. After about 15 minutes, my symptoms began to subside and I got up and answered the door for my supervisor who was a bit shocked to see me standing there shirtless. I was dazed. She didn't quite know what to say.

After I put my shirt back on, she allowed me to rest in her office for a while and we talked through what happened. Being an EMT herself, she recognized all the classic signs of a panic attack (while I had assumed I was having a heart attack at the age of 24). She sent me home for the rest of the shift and urged me to call my doctor first thing in the morning. I apologized profusely.

That job lasted about three more months. I couldn't handle the pressure of the job or the all-night shifts. And I was humiliated by the diagnosis that my coworkers had witnessed.

Mental illness is no respecter of persons. Anxiety and depression are equal opportunity employers and they do not care what kind of day or week or year you're having. And along with mental illness comes shame. Shame whispers things like "You can't get your own shit together, so stop writing." It tells lies like, "You are crazy and this will never get better."

But there is a big difference in *feeling* crazy and *being* crazy.

Living with depression means either constantly isolating yourself or always wearing a mask of performance, fearing the opinions of others, never feeling like you have it together, believing hard days will last forever. Living with depression means you know you're getting worse when nobody else has a clue. It also means feeling excited when a good day shows up out of the blue, but not sharing it with anyone because you're convinced nobody would understand or even care.

Bad days happen. Sometimes life sucks. But good days come, too. Hard days don't last forever. Take care of yourself on the hard days: eat, sleep, pray, meditate, be kind to yourself, and take your meds.

And when the good days come, lean into them and celebrate.

And the biggest thing? Stop apologizing.

When my son was a toddler, he went through a very difficult time with his stomach. Frequently, he would vomit and make major messes. Each time, he would cry. "Dada," he would say, "I'm sorry I frowed up." My son couldn't control having stomach trouble any more than I can control a panic attack in the middle of the work day. Both are inconvenient and problematic, but I wouldn't choose anxiety or depression any more than someone would willingly choose to vomit.

I've had many panic attacks since that fateful shift at the 911 center. Panic attacks don't care where you are or who you're with: at home, work, church, or driving down the road. But as miserable as they are, I have finally learned one great big truth: **I don't owe anyone an apology for my mental illness. You don't either.**

Why Self-Care Matters

As a person with mental illness, there are so many triggers I can't control — but I do have control over how I take care of myself. For me, self-care starts with getting good, solid, uninterrupted sleep. I don't stay up all hours of the night to binge on my favorite show or read just one more chapter. I find when I'm tired, my symptoms are worse.

Food matters too. I'm a busy guy, and I've never been a big breakfast eater. See how I just made two excuses? **No more excuses.** I have to take my nutrition seriously. It doesn't mean I have to join a gym, or post before and after pictures on social media. I'm just saying it's important for me to eat as healthy and as regularly as possible. It helps me feel better and get the most out of my day.

It may sound cliche' but it is absolutely true that if I don't care for yourself, no one else will. If I don't take care of myself during all phases of recovery, I am committing slow and painful emotional suicide.

The Truth About Recovery:

I have the right to take care of myself.

I have the right to seek professional help.

I have the right to rest. Take a mental health day!

I have the right to say no and stand up for myself!

I have the right to a healthy life. Health includes mind, body, and spirit.

I have the right to set clear boundaries.

I have the right to enjoy life to the fullest.

I have the right to fully acknowledge your emotions. I am not a robot.

I have the right to accept life as it comes. I don't have to have it all figured out today.

I have the right to start over.

One of the greatest ways I have begun to take good care of myself is learning to redefine the small things. This morning, a lifelong friend of our family came up to me and asked, "What's exciting in your life this week?" Without thinking, I said, "You know, most days I just want to get the kids in bed in one piece and pay the power bill. That's my main calling." I said it tongue-in-cheek, but I meant it.

As a teen and throughout my 20s, I considered everything from religion to military service to find my purpose. I wasn't sure what I was supposed to do with my life, but I was certain it would be magnificent. I was sure it would involve stages and possibly fame. I was accustomed to excelling, and didn't God promise me a hope and a future?

But last night, the magnificent showed up as my almost-2-year-old waddled over to the couch and begged, "Book, Dada, book!" For nearly an hour, my daughter laid her rosy little biscuit cheeks on my shoulder as we read *Brown Bear, Brown Bear* 47 times.

My future collides with my present when my son wants to snuggle at 1 a.m. All I really want to do is sleep in my queen-sized bed without a kid kicking my rib cage repeatedly for hours. But another thought flashes through my mind. He won't be four-years-old forever, and we won't always fit together on this twin mattress.

Where's that hope I always quoted in my 20s? It's found in the mornings I have the honor of fixing my wife's coffee while she has a few minutes of "becoming human" time on the couch. In a different season, our marriage nearly fell apart, due to my constant busyness and drive to do something big. But God's grace is greater than even our biggest mistakes. Now, I have the privilege of making her coffee and helping with household chores.

I would be lying if I said I never feel the tug of the American male, the breadwinner, to do more. Because busyness equals success, right? Those lies were deeply ingrained, but all my busyness eventually came with a price.

I'm in religious recovery now, but I'm still seeking out genuine faith.

And I notice, all the "small things" in my day are really the big things of life. The "small things" are my family. Instead of viewing my wife and children as additional baggage, one more responsibility, I now realize they are my greatest gifts. God is my hope and my children are my future. When I take my last breath on earth, won't be thinking of metrics and stats. I pray to God I won't be thinking of my failures of any sort of disappointment I ever faced, but instead of all the small things. The time I took to breathe. To kiss my son on the forehead. To reach across the kitchen table and hold my wife's hand. To notice the way a baby smells behind the ears. These tiny moments are the ones that matter the most to me now.

God isn't confined by church walls or Christian music. He isn't only impressed by preaching to an audience of 10,000. He cares just as much about my commitment to tell my children a Bible story each night. When I let go of doing big things for God, I found a God who isn't any more wowed with billboard Christianity than the single Mom who manages to put supper on the table, even if the house isn't spotless, and raise children who know their value and where they belong.

I find my hope in the fact that God connects with me on a personal level, not because of my great ability, but because of the fact that God who values who we are above what we do.

This extraordinary God is found in a thousand ordinary moments. In letting go of unrealistic expectations, I am finding God in the most wonderfully ordinary ways: at the kitchen table with my wife, working through deep-seated fears; in every intentional moment I spend with my children, cultivating their innocence and self-worth; and even on the couch at the counselor's office.

Today, I am finding God in the pew and on the playground.

Self-Compassion and Dingy Socks

It took me three days to realize I was building toward a panic attack. I think of it like a simmering pot that begs for days to boil. Eventually it will blow. Or it may finally run out of steam, still piping hot, producing nothing but exhaustion, confusion, frustration, and sticky sweat.

It reminds me of dingy socks.

My wife is a neat freak. Always has been. The house is spotless and it's not because we don't live in it. It's because she never stops cleaning. I don't know how many times a day she sweeps the floors, but I know she mops multiple times a week. Yet, no matter how much she cleans, every time I walk across the floors, the bottoms of my socks get dirty.

Anxiety is so hard to describe most of the time. It's tough to explain to those who have never experienced it. For three days, I've had that gnawing feeling in my stomach. I've been constantly checking the rearview mirror, and wishing I had a rearview mirror everywhere I go. It only goes away when I sleep, but even sleep has been light and fitful lately.

There was a time when I would question my faith whenever I felt anxious. Had I not prayed enough? Should I read another chapter of the Bible? I did tithe last week and two weeks before that, right? So why was I feeling so off? Some of my old thinking crops up during anxious times, causing me to check my bank account, assuming God is doing the exact same thing with me. I went through all the "good little church boy" items on my checklist but drew a blank. The truth is, anxiety doesn't care if you've been good or not. It's going to torment you regardless.

Anxiety is no lightweight. A friend of mine once said, "It's not your Grandma's kind of worry." Punches are thrown to the righteous and the unrighteous alike, and I've taken plenty of blows to the chin. If anything, my experience with anxiety is even *more* tumultuous when I question it from a Christian perspective. I am constantly trying to be faithful, to do all the right things, and still I walk around with that tightness that envelopes the back of my throat. Scripture promises a garment of praise for a spirit of heaviness. I think I'd like to cash in that particular promise right about now.

Yesterday, the yellow and rusting trees along the side of the road seemed to burn towards the sky. As I looked upward on my drive home, the grey skies mirrored my mood. The clouds were dingy, just like the bottoms of my white cotton socks after wearing them for a while on Lindsey's spotless floors. My soul seemed just as worn and dingy. It finally hit me that the ominous feeling I'd carried for a few days was exactly that: dingy socks.

The past few days began to make sense. Not go away. The anxiety did not dissipate, but I was able to give myself a space to breathe for a minute. I remembered that sometimes there is no explanation. Mostly, I have no control over my anxiety. There isn't always a reason why. No matter how hard I scrub at my own life, it's still there and I can't change it. I've tried medication, meditation, and breathing techniques. I've had vegetable oil crosses on my forehead and glasses of pretty good wine that manage to leave me drunk yet still just as anxious. Some of those work some of the time. Not one of them works all the time. And nothing makes it end for good.

I don't always understand His ways, but in the words of Carlos Whittaker, I do trust that "one day the suck will be less." I cannot honestly say I believe God will work ALL things for our good and for His glory. But I can trust that one day, when we leave these bodies that are prone to leukemia and Parkinson's and dementia, I believe that God will meet us in Heaven and either explain it all or His reasoning will matter less. One day, after a heartbreak, we may actually look back and say, "Look what the Lord has done." One day we may be amazed at the blessing He brought about through our suffering. But in the midst of the mess, that fact does not comfort me.

I think about the life of Jesus. God made Flesh dwelt among us and lived a fully human – and fully faithful – life during his three decades on this earth. Yet during his final days, in the Garden of Gethsemane, even Jesus said, "Hey Pops, if there is any other way, let's just high five and call this good. Because what I am experiencing and what I am about to do just plain sucks." (My paraphrase, of course).

Sometimes trusting God isn't triumphant or glorious. Sometimes trusting God isn't even a desire. It's a stubbornness that cries in the middle of the night, but attaches firmly to my faith. Sometimes trusting God isn't a praise song with the full band on a Sunday morning, but rather it's a stick-to-it-ness that says I know there is something deeper than my pain and a Power higher than anything I can rationalize, so I'll give this another shot tomorrow.

So how do I know I trust God? I go to bed at night, after an especially difficult day, week, month, life, and I am willing to wake up in the morning, willing to do it all over again. That wasn't always the case for me. There were two years when I prayed to die. Often. There were multiple times when I floored the car on the interstate, engine revving, ready to crash into the overpass in front of me. I've said before how I spent some time in ICU and on the psych ward because hard times nearly got the best of me. But I am being renewed day by day. My soul is being saved continually. I know I trust God because when the crap hits the fan, I still find peace in Him.

I never realized just how important self-care and compassion actually are until I reached the end of myself. What about you? Do you have a safe community you engage with? Are you leaning to find the balance between creating boundaries and building walls? Learning to say "no" is a powerful tool in caring for yourself. Learning to value your own mental health brings a great sense of wholeness, making you a much better contributor, in any community.

Anxiety doesn't make sense, but remaining faithful when my hands shake for no reason is what keeps me moving forward. It may still creep up my spine and whisper white noise in my ears tomorrow, but I'll also have another chance to see more of those beautiful rust-colored leaves and breathe in the crisp autumn air. Life's all about dealing with the deep things_when you're ready and taking deep breaths_every chance you get. So I'll wear my dingy socks as a badge of honor. They remind me life happens here.

If You Can't Build Walls, Make a Fence

The biggest part of self-care during my time on the ward was disconnecting from outside distractions and detractors. Before my suicide attempt, I was addicted to connection: phone, text, email, social media, blogging, radio. You name it, I was there. I had no clue what boundaries were or how they applied to my life.

On the psych ward, we couldn't have our cell phones and had specific times when we could made phone calls to our approved "safe people." We were only allowed to engage with our support system during those days. They were teaching us to reconnect with our true self.

In my 20s, I thought I needed to be 100 percent accessible 100 percent of the time. Because I had no boundaries, I had built walls that separated me from my family. I allowed the ever-present distraction of busyness to keep me from the ones who matter most. But in my time on the psych ward and in the years of therapy that have followed, I have learned that boundaries protect us all and help point us in the direction of things that truly matter.

But what do you do with the people in your life you can't completely shut out? When you can't build walls, learn to make a fence.

When I was about fifteen, Mom was cleaning out the deep freeze. There was a box of freezer-burned fish she asked me to take out to the back side of the property and bury. She emphasized that I had to bury it deep enough that the animals wouldn't dig the fish back up once it thawed.

"Sure, Mom."

I was hot, tired, and grumpy. Like any good teenager, I took that box of fish about halfway to the back of the property and covered it with some leaves. *Good enough, right?*

Wrong.

It was the middle of the summer and within just a couple of days that fish had thawed and begun to stink. About the same time, our curious little dog got out of the back fence and tore off through the woods. When she finally returned, she was dragging that box of fish in her mouth. The dog was covered from head to tail in rancid fish.

Family dynamics are a lot like dead fish on a summer day.

We expect certain people, based on their title and role in our lives, to always know how to love us well. But that's not usually the case. Those closest to us often hurt us the most. And if you choose, as I have, not to walk away from those relationships, you have to draw strong boundaries.

People can confuse emotional intimacy with honoring your parents. Your parents can love you and not know part of you. Just because a person is in your family, doesn't mean they have access to every part of your life. This is especially true in a parent-child relationship. Just because someone has the title of "Mom" or "Dad" doesn't mean they get an all-access pass to every aspect of our adult lives.

So what do you do when you're stuck?

A friend of mine recently purchased a new lake house. Everything is perfect, from the yard to the pier that leads down to the water, the screened-in back porch, and the plush living room. Everything is perfect, except the neighbors.

The neighbors are…peculiar. Interesting. Different.

They're extremely formal people. Very particular about their yard. The kind of people who take a nap daily at 1pm and put a "Do Not Disturb" sign on their front door. As my friend says it, they are "fence neighbors". There's no sitting on one another's front porches together, sharing tea or a smoke. There's no invitations for dinner. "They stay on their side of the fence and I stay on mine."

Some of us have family members who feel more like "fence neighbors". You know the ones: the mother-in-law who always has a critical opinion, the dad who never has a positive thing to say, the sister who can do everything better than you. What do you do when you can't build a wall? *You build a fence.*

It's okay to say, *"I forgive you, but I need my space."*

It's okay to say, *"I love you, but I do not want you in my life at this time."*

It's okay to say, *"I have to work through this and I don't need your help."*

It's okay to say, *"I care about you, but I will not give you the opportunity to hurt me again.*

There are some people who are fixtures in your life: the ones you don't feel you can just push away. You can check in with them and offer them the basics. You can respectfully let them know how you are doing, without divulging personal details that make you uncomfortable.

I've learned that forgiving someone doesn't mean you have to continue to be as close as you once were. If the offense cut deep, you have the right to set boundaries. You don't have to be surrounded by or deeply connected to people who don't support you. Surround yourself with people who are in your corner and believe in you.

I remember being a little boy and doing some dastardly deeds, returning later and saying "I'm sorry" and being told those infamous words, *"Sometimes sorry doesn't cut it."* Have you ever heard those words? They're true.

Just *saying* the words doesn't fix a thing.

With my mom, I apologized for not burying the box of fish, but the dog was still there, stinking up the neighborhood.

Sometimes, *sorry* doesn't cut it.

It is the same with our hearts and our minds. When you are cut to the core by something someone says or does, you cannot just take a deep breath, allow them to apologize, and move on like nothing ever happened. When my parents didn't come visit me while I was in ICU, it cut me deep, but I decided not to live like a victim forever.

People will hurt you. *Even family.* I have learned that I can say no to toxic people and take ownership of my life. And it all starts by making a fence.

Respect Bad Days

Do you ever feel anxious, discouraged, or depressed? *Me too.*

I hadn't been able to focus at work. I hadn't felt like my recent writing was connecting with my blog readers, and I was the heaviest I had ever been in my life. I needed to lose about 25 pounds. Not to mention, I had switched meds twice in six weeks and that can take a toll on your mind and emotions.

"Is that why you've been in a funk all weekend?" The question cut me deep. But she was right. I thought I had hidden it so well, but of course I can't hide from Lindsey. Sometimes I can pinpoint the reasons, but sometimes I'm just...*in a funk.*

Do you ever find yourself in that spot? In a slump? Unusually uneasy? Discouraged? Or just feeling disengaged? Maybe unmotivated?

What do you do when the flashbacks still come?

How do you respond when they are more stubborn than you ever imagined?

When you've done everything right – you've been to counseling, taken your meds, surrounded yourself with supportive people – and they still show up, what do you do?

I contacted four friends and I love the responses I received. I don't know how anyone thinks they can make it without friends. **A change in perspective can make a world of difference.**

I have another friend who always makes me laugh, so of course, I messaged him. Sometimes I don't need earth-shattering advice, I just need someone to snap me out of the vicious cycle of anxiety and tell me to stop obsessing over the negative.

One person sent me a bulleted email list of things to do, in far greater detail than I expected, but it was all such valuable feedback that I read the email three times. I am grateful for my detailed friends.

Another friend said, "I can't help with the writing but if you start working on the weight loss, I'll help." Sounds simple, right? But when I'm feeling depressed and disengaged from everyone and everything, just to hear someone say, "I'm here for you" makes me want to weep. **It helps to know I'm not alone.**

I have those days, too. I know people are here for me. But I forget to engage with them. I forget to ask for help. I forget to say, I'm bummed and I'm not sure why.

Speaking your truth defeats your shame. Part of it is shame and part of it is that life teaches us to fend for ourselves, to get over it, to stop whining. As guys, we're told if we have something to complain about, we're just being "a little bitch."

It seems that hard days are a universal experience. We can't survive on an island. Isolation is miserable, especially for someone who struggles with depression or anxiety or self-esteem issues. Finding the guts to say, "Today sucks. Can we talk?" sometimes changes everything.

I hate when I feel this way. I hate the semi-permanent knot in the back of my throat, the avoiding eye contact with co-workers and the constant urge to go home. I hate the lies that follow behind every bad day, whispering, "What a loser. Get your shit together. What's wrong with you?" I hate the shame that comes from years of being raised as a religious kid, telling me I'm not a real Christian or I wouldn't struggle so much.

But then I remember the words our pastor spoke recently, **"If it isn't good yet, God isn't finished."**

Sometimes we feel lost, stuck, frustrated, disconnected, depressed. *Funky.* Sometimes we feel anxiety because we believe the lie that says our stories don't matter. Sometimes I think I've written all there is for me to write and I might as well find a new hobby. But in those times when life feels heavy and hard, I hear God whispering, "I'm not finished yet." I hope you can hear Him, too.

I can't stop a flashback or prevent a panic attack, but by doing my best to process what has happened, I am learning to handle them a little better each time they come up.

The truth is, I am not the same desperate guy who once tried to kill myself in a hotel kitchen. The power of a second chance has changed my life. **And for me, the most important thing to remember is that a flashback is not a setback.**

I'm thankful that flashbacks aren't real. Most often, they are the darkest, scariest portions of our trauma. They are unpredictable and unfair, but I choose to keep living. Rather than allow the fear of the next flashback to hold me captive, I am choosing life. Come what may, life goes on.

The stigma of mental illness sucks. But worse is not getting better. And all any of us really want is to get better. Remember this: you are not your diagnosis. So, use your diagnosis to design a recovery plan and keep moving forward. Because mental illness is not a death sentence.

Reflecting on Four Years of Life I Never Expected to Have

September 21st is my Mulligan Day.

In golf, a mulligan is a "do-over," a chance to try the shot again. It's been four years, We definitely talk about it less around our house than we used to, but the fact that I have been given a second chance has not faded from my memory. As a friend recently said, childhood sexual abuse and a suicide attempt will always internally define me, but I am no longer defined by them externally. *Praise be to God.*

I'm alive. *What more could I possibly ask for?*

I am ALIVE! *What else matters?* Of courses other things matter, but when I consider how close we came to my wife having to bury me, the breath in my lungs and another chance at a new day seems like too much to hope for. Somebody said *the devil is in the details*, and they're right. Life has plenty of lemons to throw our way, and not all of them can be turned to lemonade, but either way, today I am alive.

For the longest time, I was inhaling and exhaling, but *I wasn't living.* I had hurts and fears and bitterness and resentment and mess that nearly killed me. *There is no medical reason for me to be here.* But I am. Not because I'm so great, but because God is. He let me live and find the life I didn't even know I had.

If the eyes are the windows to the soul, my eyes weren't empty, they were just forgetful. They had forgotten to look for the joyful things in life. I have realized that I am angry at my parents. They were young and ignorant, but they didn't ask for advice and they didn't get help for me. My Mom and Dad didn't show up when I needed them most, either after the abuse or after the suicide attempt. I am still angry at the injustice, but I cannot change what happened. What I can do now is try to look for the good in every person and situation. And if I try my hardest and cannot find anything life-giving or beneficial there, I move on.

Another thing I have learned in the past four years is to own my mistakes and the fact that they affect other people. We all mess up. We can't blame family history or former friends or employers or the government or God on the choices we make. We all make choices and sometimes we make the wrong ones. The best thing any of us can do is focus on today and the people who love us: *those who push us to be our best and love us even at our worst.* I think about my sweet Lindsey: she sat with me in the ashes, when some would have preferred that she stoke the coals. *She is the true picture of God's grace to me.*

Life is worth living. It's worth fighting through all the hard times and the dry times and the lean times and the mean times. Fight for love. Fight against the detractors that try to put your focus on anything that doesn't support you and make you better. Cut through the busyness and bullshit and figure out what on earth you're doing here. Figure out what your reason is for getting out of bed each morning…and then do *that* with all your heart. If you don't know what you're doing here, *ask.* Ask God, ask a friend who knows God. Find a counselor or therapist or get alone and get quiet and figure out what it is that makes your heart beat.

Then go and *do that.*

I'm thankful for His wonderful grace that has gotten messy with me countless times.

–Steve Austin

Resources

I'd love the opportunity to share my story, resources, and practical tools with your church, school, or civic organization. Email me at steve@iamsteveaustin.com to book a speaking engagement today!

Here's a few resources now:

1) Graceismessy.com (my blog)
2) American Foundation for Suicide Prevention
3) The Trevor Project
4) American Association of Suicidology
5) Robert-Vore.com: On Faith and Mental Health
6) TheMighty.com

I am a Recovery Rockstar:
A Self-Care Manifesto

I AM NOT *my diagnosis.* i am worthy of

I will not wall myself in.

Shame no longer gets a vote in my life.

I will not ignore my symptoms.

I will trust **I AM ALIVE.**

in a God who I will not forget how important that is.

IS constant, **I will look at the NOW**

NOT anxious. *and not the NEXT of a situation.*

I will find my reason for getting out of bed each morning. I will find what I love, and do that with all my heart.

I will respect my limits, take deep breaths, and not cause my anxiety to increase. **I will fight through** distractions, busyness, and bullshit.

I can't change it; I can live through it. **I will focus only on things that make me B E T T E R.**

The opinions of others will no longer control or define me.

IAM*STEVE AUSTIN*.COM

76395498R00063

Made in the USA
Columbia, SC
24 September 2019